The art of French Country Living

JEAN NAUDIN
COLETTE GOUVION

The art of French Country Living

HACHETTE
Illustrated

Preface

'As happy as God in France' is an old Rhineland saying to describe someone who lives life to the full. What can God possibly give France that can't be found there already? What are the delights that visitors — famous or obscure — from other countries but especially from the British Isles or the United States enjoy there? What persuades discerning celebrities such as Julian Barnes, Jim Harrison, Nancy Huston and many other writers, painters and musicians, to return constantly to France, and to linger there, staying perhaps the length of a season or for a year, but sometimes putting down roots for the rest of their lives?

The answer can be summed up as 'the art of French living', a phrase that hints at an existence that is both sensual and cultural but which turns out to be a more complex concept than it first seems. What exactly is the art of living? One answer is the practice of making time for enjoyable moments in the mundane flow of daily life. Each type of society has developed its own art of living, depending on its particular culture, climate, resources and range of life-styles. But in nearly every case what makes it distinctive are just a few elements, a certain way of being in a place; of eating; and of active and passive celebration. In some especially pleasant climates there is even an art of existence that consists of little more than allowing the place to do the living for you. But France is unique. It not only combines on its territory all possible aspects of a universal approach to life but also, in the cultural and geographical entities that are its regions, provides quite diverse expressions of the art of living which are still so balanced and consistent as to be unmistakably French. Everything plays its part: the climate; the countryside; the style of architecture; the type of culture and agriculture; the way of life; regional cooking and traditions. Each element is linked to all the others.

This art of French living is rooted in the distant past. It has been refined over the centuries, generation by generation, each making its contribution without destroying the basis on which it is built. Studying these accretions today is like decoding various layers of writing on a venerable parchment. As we become expert at this we discover all the elements of the past that combine to create the present. It may become clear that the art of living well has survived to some extent in cities, but it has often become buried under transient fashions which have nothing in common with it. Essentially, however, it is the fruit of practices brought from the provinces not so long ago, when France was predominantly rural. The art of French living is derived from the French peasantry. It is unashamedly based on life as lived in the country, in the finest sense.

In fact, to take the best advantage of its geography, climate and natural resources, each region gradually developed particular ways of building, cultivating the land, arranging space and using local products which made life easier for the inhabitants as well as more agreeable. Where can we find this art of living today in forms that reveal it as intrinsic to France, in spite of all the gentle accommodations of modernity? The answer lies in the countryside, where nature is still omnipresent, and nuance counts for more than dramatic gestures; moderation is more important than excess; good sense more than the latest fad; know-how more than brash achievements; and tranquillity more important than feverish activity.

In short, the classic art of living is still valued in the country, along with the wisteria twined over bowers, dahlias bordering vegetable gardens, and hollyhocks growing round garden sheds. Together with their vines and traditional dishes, it is cherished in those *départements* that refuse to be categorised by numbers, instead remaining known by name: Poitou, Touraine, Anjou, Brittany, Alsace, Normandy, Provence, Picardy and Languedoc. If you take to their hidden roads and wander down their footpaths you will stumble on this way of life without really looking for it. In order to really understand it you must imbibe it slowly, share its rituals, and savour its aromas and its pleasures one by one. The foreign visitors who do this are on the right track, like the English novelist Julian Barnes, whose *Something to Declare* contains an affectionate celebration of rural France: 'My automatic images of being in France are initially pastoral: quiet canals lined with trees as regular as comb-teeth; a hunched bridge across shallow, pebbly water; dormant vines resting their flayed arms on taut wires.... And when my images stop being pastoral, they do not change much in key: not to Paris or the larger cities or some yelping exhibitionist beach, but to quiet working villages with rusting café tables, lunchtime torpor, pollarded plane-trees, the dusty thud of boules and an all-purpose *épicerie*....'

A murmuring river; a green hillside; a café terrace beneath the plane trees; a provincial bedroom scented with lavender; a kitchen fragrant with the aroma of poultry roasting on the embers and cakes browning in the oven; a truly convivial meal around a table bearing a carefully preserved tablecloth embroidered by a grandmother or great-grandmother, and good wine joyously shared: such are the images contributing to a sense of happiness that might be called God-given. These things are treasured in France, and we can treasure them too.

Seductive landscapes

Whether in Burgundy or Languedoc, the Auvergne or the Loire, the most typically French landscapes share two characteristics: a gentle ability to soothe the spirit and perfect civility. The topographical relief and the climate forged their distinctive outlines, but then each feature has been moulded and cultivated by human hand. This is nature adapted to meet human needs. Here the passing seasons change colour, and time flows at its own pace. In these landscapes you can be happily alone and, at the same time, enjoy being amidst signs of life. No two regions have the same sky, the same clouds, the same rounded curves, or the same colouration, yet all share a similar harmony. You can fall in love with them all, or treat just one as your Promised Land.

LEFT
The ponds of Dombes, in the Ain, are carefully cultivated and maintained. They are emptied every year giving the locals an opportunity to fish for an abundance of carp and pike.

It is possible to enjoy strolling in the French countryside without any particular goal, walking just for pleasure and to relish the peace. But be prepared to be stopped in your tracks at some point on your route. Some unexpected sight may surprise you as you descend a hillside, come to a bend of a pathway, or reach the edge of a wood. You may come across a landscape framed like a painting, and fall in love with it, seduced by its sheer proportions, perfect lighting, and elegant natural appearance. It may be a small valley complemented by the undulations of a cheeky river that detains you. On the other hand, on the way up a mountain you may reach a plateau on which the sky seems to rest, and where sheep are peacefully nibbling the wild grasses. Or you may be arrested by the sight of a green meadow under flowering apple trees. Whatever spot delights you will surely fit the definition of the writer, Antoine Furetière: 'Landscape: the territory which extends as far as the eye can see'; and this may be the one with which you fall in love immediately.

Where in France you find your ideal landscape, is a question of your personal affinities and knowledge of the country. There are hundreds of areas in France that offer human dimensions, subtle variations and peaceful harmony. If you study the landscape carefully you will see that agriculture plays a major role. There are said to be more than six hundred different agricultural traditions in France. Your understanding of the relationship between land and farming will benefit from more prolonged and highly-nuanced acquaintance with it.

As with all burgeoning love affairs, appearance plays a role. You appreciate the outlines, a prospect opening out to the horizon or disclosing a gentle slope. Your eyes feast on the colours of the sky, the passing clouds, the earth, the vegetation, or the warm-toned tiles, the blue-tinged slates or grey roofing stones on an isolated house, or perhaps a group of houses huddled together in a village and the sudden thrust of a church tower towards heaven. The dominant colours serve to identify a region, and the

ABOVE
The fertile land of the Gers,
with the snow-capped Pyrenees
in the background.

RIGHT above
A Drôme landscape near
Saint-Roman.

RIGHT below
Harvest in the hills of Lauragais,
a French equivalent of Tuscany,
between Toulouse and Carcassone.

palette is richly varied and endlessly shifting. It changes according to the weather, the light, and the season. Rain varnishes the picture. The sun sometimes heightens, and sometimes obscures, tonalities. A covering of frost or snow has a magical effect, turning the landscape into a basic design on which only the main shapes are delineated. March brings fresh green shoots, summer yellows, and autumn, blazing golds.

Sight is far from being the only sense to be seduced. The range of aromas is as rich as that of colours, and varies according to region, climate, type of weather and even time of day. From the end of winter, violets broadcast their delicate scent. In spring, waysides are fragrant with the scent of acacias, and elderberry flowers add perfume to the ruins that this shrub swiftly colonises. Within a single landscape area, for instance, to the south of the Loire, you can detect the smell of pines here, lavender there, as well as wild box and thyme, while shafts of sunlight strike stony paths and release the characteristic odour of hot rocks and flints. In meadow landscapes at the height of the summer,

RIGHT above
The Lot meanders peacefully between green banks before joining up with the Garonne and the Dordogne to form the Gironde estuary, downstream from Bordeaux.

RIGHT below
Haymaking in a corner of the Drome which anticipates some of the features of Provence.

dawn brings the smell of fresh grass and twilight, the scent of hay. Broom triumphs in regions of moorland. The smell of wild mint is supremely attractive around brooks, streams, and rivers. In woodlands, autumnal mists and rains mix the exhalations of earth, ferns and mushrooms and, close to human habitation, the odour of wood smoke. Thus each landscape has its own visual and olfactory markers. Then there are the sounds: the murmuring or lapping of flowing water; the minor music of springs; the gentle sighs of reeds swaying in the breeze; the howling of the wind; the jangling of cowbells; the throbbing of agricultural machinery; and chimes from church or belfry, complete the rich picture of a living landscape.

But things seen, breathed and heard will not alone convey the deeper meaning of a landscape. They are merely those aspects of its immense complexity which our senses can apprehend, 'the photographically detectable nature of geographic reality', in the words of historian, Jean-Robert Pitte in his book, *Histoire du paysage français* (History of the French Landscape).

What lies behind this 'cinematic reality'? An outcrop of rock, a climate, a landscape, a water feature? These are the raw materials on which humans have relied to arrange the way in which they live. By trial and error, each type of soil has given rise to specific modes of agriculture, such as viniculture, wheatfields and animal husbandry. Above all, the inhabitants of any particular area have used local materials — stone, wood, earth and vegetation — to construct their homes. Geography and climate have dictated the sites where people have settled or whether they have chosen to live individually or in groups, as well as determining the layouts and shapes of the houses that will ensure that they enjoy a degree of security and comfort. In places where they were the only means of transport, rivers and waterways allowed goods and people to move around. But all of this required many years' hard work, altering and improving the environment.

Although they have a deceptive appearance of gracious spontaneity, the landscapes of the French countryside are not natural. Quite the reverse. They are profoundly civilised, and it is this that makes them both pleasing and reassuring. Two hundred generations have laboured on the land from the Neolithic period — this has yielded evidence of the earliest known human agriculture — to the present. They have cleared the fields; conquered new areas for cultivation; opened up paths; drained marshes; created dykes and altered water courses; cut down or replanted forests; reforested the moors; built ramparts; constructed villages

BELOW
When the Renoir family lived in Les Collettes they would often walk to the Arc, in the hinterland of Cannes.

RIGHT
Near Saint-Omer, in the Pas de Calais, the Aa, which means 'water' in Old Germanic, goes peacefully on its way towards the North Sea. Its calm waters make it an ideal environment for the favourite French sport of angling.

and towns; and built bridges. Not a century, nor even a decade, has gone by without its inhabitants remodelling the environment, often with intelligence, with moderation and with an instinct for proportion and harmony.

As Jean-Robert Pitte also says: 'The countryside expresses human material needs in terms of their more or less effective means of transforming nature. It also reflects human culture (in the sense of "instruction", "knowledge" and also "imagination"). It also points explicitly to the gamut of human needs: how we feed ourselves, consume other products and services, possess and express a certain conception of social justice, defend ourselves, meet, come together, communicate with one another with respect to certain cosmological or religious values.'

You find the same approach in the work of the semiologist Roland Barthes, who sees the landscape as 'the richest of signs'. Born of a sometimes turbulent but always passionate union between nature and culture, French landscapes are diverse yet authentic expressions of a civilisation whose fruit is the 'art of living'.

LEFT
The church of Saint-Grégoire de Ribeauvillé, among the Alsatian vineyards.

ABOVE
Half-timbered house nestling at the edge of a wood in Calvados.

PREVIOUS DOUBLE-PAGE SPREAD left
The Charolais is still the best breed of cattle in France for meat production.

RIGHT above
Plump sheep enjoy the wild, scented grasses of the Auvergne hills under the watchful eye of their shepherd.
In the Drôme (below),
sheep are one of the mainstays of the local economy. Each year they follow the seasonal migration routes.

ABOVE AND RIGHT
At Saugues, in the Upper Loire,
this café with its traditional
façade is the main meeting-place
for young and old on market days.

DOUBLE-PAGE SPREAD overleaf
The village of Saugues lies
stretched out under the sky,
firmly anchored to its granite
plateau. Villagers still tell the
legend of the mysterious beast
of Gévaudan that terrorised the
area in the eighteenth century.

Architectural harmonies

The architecture, as much as the landscape, gives you an indication of which region of France you are in. The regional style of architecture can be observed in the grand country houses, the manor houses and the unpretentious workmen's cottages. Wherever it appears, it will be the product of a rich understanding of the earth on which it stands, and it will have been erected by skilled builders with excellent taste and knowledge of local traditions. The materials come from nearby: yellow stone, sombre shale, granite, pink brick, oak timbers, and hot-coloured tiles or blue-tinged roof-stones. Tradition and experience dictate that builders follow the rules of harmony and proportion, and ensure that each house is appropriate to the climate and to the life-styles of the inhabitants. It is always a pleasure to live in such buildings which seem to grow naturally from the landscapes in which they are set.

A village of cosily arranged houses; a detached country house in a garden designed to please the eye; a farmhouse with squat outbuildings stretching along a pot-holed track – such structures are so much part of their environment that they seem to be almost an expression of it. The various building styles of France offer an excellent means of developing an understanding of the art of living.

If you want to identify the art of French living, it is best to begin not in the superb châteaux, which have their own kind of architecture and life-styles, but in a more modest home, more obviously related to its surroundings. The main types are the country seats, farms, mills and village houses. There are some rare instances of late medieval buildings, but otherwise the oldest existing traditional houses date from the sixteenth century. There are many examples from the prolific period of house construction between 1760 and 1860, while the most recent of these traditional houses date from the late nineteenth century. However old they are, they seem similar to the eye and, apart from a few minor differences of height and quality of materials, form a homogeneous unity in each region.

This unity of architectural style can make the appearance of such homes the most distinctive feature of a certain age – even more than the landscape, name or any other aspect of their *département*. It did not occur by chance. These houses were built by local builders and craftsmen, not by ambitious architects anxious to make a grand statement. They followed a type of construction and materials sympathetic to local conditions, and few would have dreamt of changing building methods that had stood the test of time.

The styles are immensely varied across France. There is not a single region – or even micro-region – that has not acquired a unique mode of its own. The interplay of outlines and size changes so that hanging roofs peculiar to snowy regions can also be seen in areas with very dry summers when the smallest raindrop must be saved. Low-slung buildings are typical of Brittany and Normandy

where the buildings seem to cling to the ground for greater protection from the winds. The wheat plains of northern France generally feature squat farms, while flat roofs are often seen in Mediterranean areas.

This variety has arisen from the wealth of natural materials, obligingly provided by the country's rich geology. Wood was traditionally used for the framework and the foundations; also for the weather-boarding on mountain chalets, and above all in the half-timbered houses of Normandy, Alsace and the Basque country. Wood is seldom used by itself for walls, but is combined with brick in the northern regions and in Aquitaine, with rammed clay in Normandy and the region around Lyons, or with cob. As well as being an invaluable structural material, wooden decoration gives a region a particular identity. Simple chevrons and vertical rhythms are found in Normandy, squares and rectangles crossing at oblique angles are found in eastern France, whereas chequer-work is typical of the Basque country. Similarly, clay is used for bricks, whether baked or unbaked, and – depending on the

oxide content and baking temperature – they can range in colour from brown to golden pink via a strong red.

Finally, many types of stone are used, from Breton granite to the grey sandstone of the Languedoc and the red sandstone of the Vosges, the light calcareous tufa of the Loire to the millstone of the Parisian basin. Stone walls may be made of undressed rubble or of precisely-cut blocks, skilfully balanced, as in the dry stone walls of Provence or the Languedoc, or pointed using a cement coating made of local sand. The end result is often an incidental beauty. The most interesting façades of this regional architecture combine different materials in surprising ways, mixing bricks with sandstone, or adding friezes of river-bed pebbles set in relief.

These colourful walls are topped with tiles in ochres and subtle pinks, bluish-grey slate, or roof stones of dull grey. Thinking about the wealth of colour and building materials in France, it is easy to see how the designer Jean-Philippe Lenclos came up with the title of his book, *Géographie des couleurs de la France* (Geography of the Colours of France).

Enclosures, gates, paths, terraces, staircases, steps, arbours and pergolas complement the local architectural styles, and connect the outdoors tactfully and pleasingly with the stylish interiors. Gates and enclosures may be seen as frontiers between public space and the private domain, and play a considerable symbolic and aesthetic role in the complex unity of building and landscape. They often follow local building styles, are made of the same materials – stone, rubble, brick, sandstone or cob – and may even be topped with small roofs. Then nature lends a hand. Stone walls may be invaded by moss and wild flowers, making them so attractive that they resemble sculptures that demand to be touched. The traditional hedge, more modest than the stone wall, compensates for its lack of solidity with soft outlines and provides a haven for birdsong, while wooden fences humbly and discreetly define the limits of a property.

Variations and idiosyncratic features added by the owner do not detract in the least from the charm of these houses which will share a fundamental style common to their region and type of construction.

LEFT
The simplicity of the Château de Montvert, in the Dordogne, is a perfect example of seventeenth-century Perigord house-building.

BELOW
An eighteenth-century house on the banks of the Dordogne, restored and raised in the nineteenth-century to protect it from flooding.

DOUBLE-PAGE SPREAD overleaf
A meadow with grazing sheep emphasizes the striking effect of the prestigious Château de Miromesnil in Normandy.

LEFT

Château du Bosc, near Camjax,
in the Aveyron (midi-Pyrénées),
one of the houses of the artist
Toulouse-Lautrec.

RIGHT

A view on the Dordogne at
Saint-Seurin-de-Prats. The
river wends its way dreamily,
offering a romantic reflection
of foliage in the park.

DOUBLE-PAGE SPREAD *overleaf*

Monumental architecture under
snow: a winter view of the Château
de Brécy in Calvados (Normandy),
a design attributed to François
Mansart.

There may be paved or tiled terraces, lined with flower
pots, some steps where children love to sit, and seats for
casual evening conversation: these are signs of a certain
way of life. Who can resist the appeal of grapes ripening on
a trellis, a pergola covered with fragrant wisteria, or a façade
that is home to climbing roses?

Their various aspects, expensive or modest but never ugly
or vulgar, make such houses 'living homes' rich with traces
of the lives of former residents. From one end of France to
the other, they share a quality that the architect Robert
Hubrecht charmingly called 'affability'. Perhaps that is
why they provide an atmosphere and setting so admirably
suited to fulfilling human needs and inclinations.

RIGHT
The sandy pathway and yellow
façade of the little Château de
Saint-Émilion, near Bordeaux,
add to its tranquil grace.

BELOW
The blue shutters and white
walls of a house in the Dordogne
seem to sparkle amid the mixed
green of the park.

DOUBLE-PAGE SPREAD overleaf
A traditional Provençal house.
Here nothing feels pretentious
and details such as the stones
furrowed by entwining vegetation
and the collection of quirky pots
declare that whoever lives here
loves life.

ABOVE
In the Aveyron, a carefully worked
stone façade, with pillars that
are both calculated and discreet,
shows typical restraint.

RIGHT
The garden of Paul Cézanne's
studio in Aix-en-Provence
features an old staircase
assailed by wayward vegetation.

BELOW
Majestic plane trees and a gravel
path lead to the Jas de Bouffan,
a property belonging to the
Cézanne family and situated on
the outskirts of Aix-en-Provence.

RIGHT above
The estate of the Collettes seen
through the olive trees. Auguste
Renoir bought the property to
save the trees which were about
to be destroyed. The house now
contains a museum dedicated to
the painter.

RIGHT below
The mossy staircase of a little
château near Bordeaux.

LEFT
Every detail contributes to the
seductive power of a place: the
edge of a stone water butt and
the old jar are both tasteful
and attractive.

ABOVE
If you push the plain wooden,
painted wicket-gate, you will
find yourself on the river bank
without leaving the estate.

DOUBLE-PAGE SPREAD overleaf
A frost-covered corner of a
garden in the Gers. In spring,
the leaves will return to the
trees and once again, under
their shade, the rustic table and
bench will host alfresco meals.

Cultivated gardens

An old saying holds that the inside of a house belongs to its owners and the outside to passers-by. However, this is not entirely true of gardens. The visual pleasure of gardens is as important for the passing visitor as for the owner whose garden is an extension of his or her house. Ownership of a garden brings with it the power to decide how the garden will look and what activities will take place within it. Gardeners enjoy watching the passing seasons and experiencing the joy of planting and harvesting their flowers. They are always anxious to make the most of their gardens so that life outside of the house is as pleasurable as that within. Gardening as an art consists of constantly adding lyrical touches and mood-enhancing notes to change and improve the feeling of the plot, and this is the case whether the garden is large or small, or contains spectacular flower-beds, fragrant rose-gardens, or vine-covered terraces.

One does not necessarily have to cross the threshold to decide whether a house would be a good place to live. The garden offers a foretaste of the whole by the way in which it is tended: its charm and its display of imagination and invention. Whether large and well-designed or small and quaint, a garden can complement a property and enhance it spiritually; wonderful gardens are the result of a long love-affair between the French and their houses.

This romance began with the Romans, in so many ways the ancestors of the French of today. During their expansion to the east in the first century BC, they discovered the Egyptian garden, itself heir to a tradition born on the banks of the Tigris and the Euphrates more than five thousand years ago. Regular, well-designed yet somehow voluptuous, Egyptian gardens perfectly matched the Roman taste for order and beauty, and many horticultural ideas and plants were taken from Egypt to Italy. Roman town houses thereafter acquired attractive gardens that afforded their owners spectacles of delight, and rich citizens living in big suburban villas recalled their rural origins by planting vegetables, medicinal herbs, and fruit and ornamental trees. In Gaul, wealthy Gallo-Romans followed the same styles. The Roman empire eventually declined and the taste for gardens died out too but, like a river disappearing into the ground only to re-emerge somewhere else, it eventually grew up again in the austere monastery gardens of the Middle Ages, cultivated primarily for nutritional ends. Later, these monastic enclosures were also planted with lilies and roses for the laudable purpose of decorating church altars and enhancing feast-days.

Although the gardens of the West had fallen into a deep decline, those of the Byzantine world maintained the tradition of Roman sumptuousness, and the Arabs too took arboriculture, horticulture and the art of making gardens to new heights of sophistication. The Crusades brought French knights into contact with these traditions for the first time as they passed through Cyprus, Damascus and

ABOVE
Doorway to the walled garden
of the Château de Miromesnil.

RIGHT HAND PAGE
A lawn leads to beautiful trees
which provide refreshing shade,
and lovingly tended hortensias
grow along the low brick wall.
This private garden near Toulouse
is the pride and joy of its owner.

Constantinople; and the Crusaders returned home with new plants and the idea of a garden as a place of paradise, and they tried to recreate their settings so they could enjoy similar delights. The rustic courtyards of feudal aristocrats were now covered with banks of greenery, arbours, ornamental flowers and trees, and before long the link with the gardens of Roman Gaul had been restored.

Each historical period adopted its own style. The kings, queens, favourites, princes and the grandest cardinals led the way. The aristocracy followed, then – not wanting to be left behind – the bourgeoisie. Italian Renaissance gardens were succeeded by a fashion for mazes, then successively Baroque fantasies; Classical parks with spectacular prospects; Romantic designs; English gardens and rose gardens; and the designer gardens of the present day.

The garden gradually became an external sign of wealth and knowledge. Francis Bacon, the English philosopher of the seventeenth century, observed that at times when politeness and elegance are cherished, men first erect magnificent buildings and then lay out beautiful gardens, since gardens symbolise an even greater perfection. This pattern was true of France too. Gardens became supremely important and detailed rules and regulations were devised for their designers.

Jacques Boyceau de la Béraudière, Louis XIII's Superintendent of the Royal Gardens in the early seventeenth century, published a *Treatise on Gardening in accordance with the Principles of Nature and the Rules of Art*. It included gardening hints, plant catalogues and even patterns for embroideries with plant designs. Well-to-do homes adopted a strict division between the showy flower garden and the functional vegetable garden: the former was to the front of the house and, as 'the' garden, enjoyed precedence over the practical plot tucked away at a suitable distance from the house. But vegetable gardens too could become masterpieces, as demonstrated in the kitchen garden at Versailles, designed by La Quintinie. Later designers were keen to intellectualize the concept of gardening. At the end of the eighteenth century, Claude-

Nicolas Ledoux, architect of the Royal Saltworks at Arc-et-Senans near Besançon, conceived a plan that then seemed revolutionary: an ideal city where every house would be surrounded by its own garden. The French philosophers, Jean-Jacques Rousseau and Voltaire, had already advocated gardens which would promote an appreciation of nature and be enjoyed as an expression of natural wisdom, as a place of tranquillity, and as a means of educating the lower orders. They attacked the rectilinear patterns of Classical gardens, praised the use of curves and casual harmony in garden design, and thought of gardens as a way of expressing their political and philosophical ideas.

In the twenty-first century, gardens are more fashionable than ever. They offer a host of different styles and emphases, and are the heirs of all the experiments and developments of gardeners of the past. Gardens are minor worlds of pleasure, whether they are expensively maintained Classical parks or examples of the natural profusion of the English cottage garden; whether they combine flowers and vegetables or hide exquisite, gently tended nooks; whether they offer a host of scents and colours or restrained planting in secluded enclosures in the manner of monastic gardens.

LEFT
A garden in the Gers is transfigured by the almost exotic appearance of dense yet sparkling clumps of irises.

ABOVE left
Framed by the luxuriant vegetation of the Virginia creeper, one sees the welcoming smile of the owner of the house in the Limousin countryside.

ABOVE right
A farm dog offers an equally friendly face at this farm in the Gers.

PAGES 60-61

In this cottage garden in the Aveyron, there is little space yet flowers are omnipresent, joyously mixed and succeeding one another at regular intervals from spring to the end of autumn. Their glory adds a blaze of colour to every stone corner, stairway, step or fountain edge.

PAGES 62-63

From one château to the next, their parks show the stages of the evolution of the landscape gardener's art. Courances, in the Île-de-France (left), with its plane- trees and its canals, is one of the most beautiful examples of seventeenth-century Classical gardens. Its creation preceded the more famous gardens of Versailles and Vaux-le-Vicomte in the Loire. The symmetry of its pathways and flowerbeds contrasts with the graceful freedom of nineteenth-century English parks (right).

PAGES 64-65

At Bonnieux in Provence, mineral and vegetable combine in gentle curves. A free variation on an Italian theme.

LEFT

Under a trellis in the Corrèze in the Dordogne, a terrace of sophisticated paving-stones sports a bench for idle gossip and has room for a table on which lime blossom dries in the midday sun.

RIGHT

In the Dordogne, a summer dining-area under the shade of the trees awaits its guests.

PREVIOUS DOUBLE PAGE
Open-air meals: a familiar
ritual enjoyed by young and
old in this enclosed garden
in south-western France.

LEFT-HAND PAGE
A collection of chubby cactus
plants grow happily in a
sheltered spot by a wall.

RIGHT-HAND PAGE
A table is laid for lunch, on
a stone plinth in a Provençal
garden, with the same care as it
would be in a dining-room in the
house. An old wooden side-table
is perfect for serving the pudding.

PAGES 72-73 AND 74-75
This table, laid beneath flowering
apple trees, recalls the meals
and snacks enjoyed by novelist
Marcel Proust while on holiday
in the Normandy seaside resort
of Cabourg.

PAGES 76-77
A fringed hammock slung
between two trees is an invitation
to relax in summer tranquillity.
It evokes not only the delights
of a siesta spent swinging gently
from side-to-side, but also dreamy
thoughts, memories of childhood
happiness and the pleasures of
reading with no time pressures.

Atmospheric halls and living-rooms

Hallways, whether elegant or relaxed, never fail to disclose the kind of welcoming atmosphere intended by the owner. Halls set the tone and the living-room emphasises and extends it. The choice of objects dotted about the house – flower arrangements, furniture, fabrics, lamps and the intimate corners in the vast reception rooms of magnificent old-world châteaux – reveals the taste and attitude of the owners of the house. Sometimes a charming disorder, even in rooms where the real living goes on, can quite upset the planned overall order. More often, however, a jumble of styles can evoke the successive generations that have added their unique touches without effacing those of their forebears. The effect can be so convincing that the visitor is seized with an overwhelming desire to wallow in the atmosphere of these rooms.

LEFT
The hallway in Claude Monet's house in Giverny reveals much about the character of the owner, his genius and good nature, and the stress he placed on simplicity, unpretentiousness and harmony.

ABOVE

In a house in the Dordogne,
this unassuming early
twentieth-century coat-rack
forms part of the decorative
whole.

RIGHT

Floor-tiles in Proust's family
home in Illiers-Combray.
The motif, strong colours
and gleaming silky finish
are typical of the tiled hallways
in middle-class houses of the
end of the nineteenth and early
twentieth centuries.

The front door opens to reveal the inside of the house, and
some entrance halls offer a welcome without much fuss.
In such cases, the everyday atmosphere of living-rooms
can exude a compelling charm that the formality of grand
reception rooms can never match.

Like gardens, the most captivating halls and living-rooms
reflect the personalities, histories and memories of their
owners. Provided that they are not sacrificed on the high
altar of fashion or stripped in obedience to some exacting
aesthetic idea, they reveal the personal taste of their
present owners as it complements the past. This or that
piece of furniture may date from the distant or recent
past, some fabrics or cushions are contemporary, and
occasional objects and ornaments are of indeterminate
age, and come from a variety of places; but the ensemble
seems to have been there always, pleasing the eye and
adding to the familiarity that is an essential part of the art
of living. This art of living avoids the phoney stage-sets of
stylish interior decorating magazines, for the dreams it
evokes are of the actual houses of painters and writers, and
it entices the visitor with beautiful things inherited or
acquired by chance, with unpretentious images, and with
everyday objects. Your attention is drawn to a battered
armchair or a sofa that has seen better days but is still
welcoming, and to an utterly charming scatter of books,
plants and flowers. You can see examples of rooms like this
in the houses once lived in by writers like Colette, Joseph
Delteil and Gaston Bachelard, and painters like Matisse
and Picasso.

From the moment you enter the house, the hall sets the
tone. Halls often have beautiful floors, and offer an inkling
of the entire interior design of the house. Builders, though,
know that they are passages between inside and out, and
likely to suffer comings and goings, muddy or grassy boots,
and water dripping from umbrellas, so they often try to
create a strong, solid, but attractive passage-way. They
have called on the durability and charm of large flagstones
superbly cut and well laid; black-and-white stone tiles

with decorative inserts and borders; marble, as in the most famous châteaux;, more commonly, baked-clay or red hexagonal floor tiles; and, in more recent houses, decorated ceramic tiles. Today all these inherited delights are well-maintained and scrubbed with care. On these floors you may find luxuries of a kind often unknown in modern houses: the functional and the beautiful or unusual are found side-by-side yet never look out of place. A mundane coat-rack may accommodate boots, garden clogs or mules, but also a piece of sculpture; and you may find a telephone beside a Persian miniature on a side-table.

Today's living-rooms rarely obey the old rule which decreed that they should hold just one type of furniture. Instead the owner-designer's inspiration is that everything should be chosen for its intrinsic attractiveness. Fashion does not regulate choice, and no one house resembles another. Sometimes you can detect a faint local influence in the presence of a piece of regional furniture, or a certain arrangement of objects ordained by a beautiful fireplace or window embrasure in situ. The rest is a matter of personal taste, and the owners are the decision-makers of their own kingdom. Nevertheless, a close inspection may disclose the features that produce the winning atmosphere. It may be waxed, polished, and irresistibly fragrant wooden floors reflecting the play of sunlight; a lamp, candles and a fire in the hearth; or slightly worn and faded rugs and carpets, finely-toned and there to be walked on and not avoided as too precious for practical purposes.

The furniture, whether fine antiques or more modest pieces, is usually old and looks well-worn. No care is taken to renovate it and its imperfections are tolerated. Here the mixing of styles and period is not a social or aesthetic crime. A Louis XVI chest of drawers may be displayed alongside a Louis-Philippe games table, and a Voltaire armchair is paired with a Napoleon III sofa. The overriding idea is the harmony of the colour scheme. Yet some of these pieces may be heirlooms handed down for generations, often remaining under the same roof for many centuries, imbibing memories as the years pass. In such a room one can imagine a modern young woman curled up in an armchair that belonged to a grandparent, headphones on and reading quietly. Her daughter is practising scales on a piano that has known a succession of little fingers somewhat clumsily attempting a Chopin nocturne, a Beethoven sonata, or Mozart's *Turkish March*. Of course, these pieces of furniture could have been acquired as the result of a lover's chance request here, or an antique dealer's or secondhand-shop offer there. Perhaps the owner fell in love with first one, then another. Their history may be unknown to you, but you can always endow them with one, for one of the pleasures of the imagination is to give worn though beautiful objects a new existence.

Such furniture, however attractive and charming, is not the only element determining atmosphere. Also important are details that reveal the owners' taste, breadth of imagination, freedom of spirit or sense of well-being. Here again there are no rules. The spirit of a place is unique according to the elements of which it is made up: French windows, hung with beautiful thick curtains, open onto the garden; lamps and candelabra emit a gentle light; the fireplace is always ready for logs to crackle and sparkle; mirrors are judiciously positioned to play delightful games with space; half-read magazines wait to be taken up again from occasional tables, and here and there are cups of tea or half-filled glasses; old books are stacked up or scattered about. All these things are elements of the day-by-day art of living.

The same happy juxtaposition applies to furnishings, ornaments and occasional objects — a note of colour and relaxation is provided by cushions softening the appearance of the sometimes rather stiff armchairs and bringing comfort to sofas and wing chairs. They may be plain or decorated, covered with fine tapestry-work, with precious fabrics, or with a plain cotton fabric. Similar effects are achieved with rugs, covers and throws scattered here and there. These can be rustic or sophisticated, old or contemporary.

RIGHT
The door forms a pleasing frame
for the main avenue of Château
Soutard, in Saint-Émilion.

Bric-a-brac and memorabilia are distributed around the room in enjoyable disorder, and cleverly serve to unify the feeling of the whole. An African statue may stand next to an antique terracotta horse, or a woven basket from the Central Pacific. An old adze chosen for its texture and form may be placed beside a Khmer Buddha and a contemporary sculpture. A silver frame may counterpoint a tortoiseshell box or complement a precious porcelain plate; no conjunction is alien. A collection of objects such as this may be grouped together merely because they are loved, but they operate as grace-notes which emphasise and personalise the general harmony of a room.

The visitor may notice the ubiquitous flower arrangements which are an essential part of creating this kind of atmosphere. Foliage, sprigs and branches from a forest are mixed with flowers from garden or market. The results may not rival the haughty compositions of grand florists, but they are always rich with freshness and charm. In a sense, they make up the centrepiece of informal drawing rooms, essentially designed to be comfortably lived in.

LEFT-HAND PAGE
In the morning light, two ancient Chinese terracotta horses guard the entrance hall of a château in Provence

RIGHT
Even a haphazard scene like these unmatched, yet attractive, plates with scarves and overcoats hung above them on simple clothes hooks, can be a joy to behold after coming in from the garden.

LEFT AND RIGHT
Whether sophisticated or rustic, hung over a fireplace or on a wall, mirrors enlarge the space of a room, maximise light and add a touch of mystery.

PAGE 88
Set apart by printed curtains, the writer's corner, with its bunches of flowers, ornaments and family photographs, is an inviting place to write (Château de Courances).

PAGE 89
Soft furnishings, tapestries and fabrics encourage relaxation and daydreaming.

ABOVE
In the Château de Montvert,
in the Dordogne, the light tones
of the soft cushions on the wicker
armchair, create a comfortable
place to put one's feet up.

RIGHT
In the Château du Bosc, in
the Aveyron, a vase of lilies
on the fine console table and
a tapestry in the background,
form a still-life composition
(Toulouse-Lautrec's house).

ABOVE

In a drawing-room in south-western France, a rare Austrian double-keyboard piano made by Ignaz Pleyel (1757–1831). This collector's item would fill amateur collectors of these four-handed instruments with envy.

RIGHT

The world of the Proustian salon is conjured up in this scene with the score of the operetta *Ciboulette*, a reminder of the long-standing friendship between its composer, Reynaldo Hahn, and the writer.

DOUBLE-PAGE SPREAD *overleaf*

The choice of materials helps to create the ambiance of a living-room. Wood, terracotta tiles and stone create an atmosphere of tranquillity and comfort.

LEFT AND RIGHT
Armchairs always find their
natural place, whether in front
of fireplaces, round occasional
tables or in window bays.
Their style may vary, classical
or nineteenth-century, clad
in dignified fabrics or draped
in soft velvet.

FOLLOWING DOUBLE-PAGE
SPREADS
An assortment of books, old,
new and misplaced from the
library, invades this space.
They add a unique atmosphere
to this country house or to the
Château du Bosc at Camjac.
A mischievous boy called
Toulouse-Lautrec lived in the
house, which is owned by his
family, and is a museum to him.
His early drawings are exhibited
in one of the rooms.

9

8

ROUSSE
ENSUEL
LUSTRÉ

LAROUSSE
MENSUEL
ILLUSTRÉ

H. MARTIN

H. MARTIN

H. MARTIN

1

2

4

HISTOIRE
DE
FRANCE

HISTOIRE
DE
FRANCE

HISTOIRE
DE
FRANCE

32-1934

1929-1931

PETIT

LEFT
Books are carefully arranged
to calm the spirit in the
drawing-room of a provincial
château. To calm the body,
there is a bowl of lime-flower
tisane and a madeleine of the
kind that Marcel Proust
mentioned in his novel
À la recherche du temps perdu
(Remembrance of Things Past).

DOUBLE-PAGE SPREAD overleaf
A nineteenth-century Chinese
dress, carelessly thrown over
a Second Empire sofa with
its wrought-metal frame
and Paisley-patterned fabric,
displays its silken splendour.

Tranquil bedrooms

Imagine a provincial bedroom and you will probably conjure up a haven insulated from the hurly-burly of modern life. It may contain an antique four-poster bed, pretty counterpane, quilted eiderdown and fresh linen sheets. The scent of lavender and lilies wafts from the wardrobe and chest of drawers. There is a bedside table with familiar objects, and a book with a bookmark inserted at the page where the sleepy reader closed it. The room contains family memorabilia, shutters that exclude the night but open to the dawn, and all-in-all it conveys a benign feeling of well-being.

Such rooms may suddenly evoke a childhood dream of the kind that lies dormant in so many adults. You may suddenly be seized with a fierce longing and mad desire to stay put for a while or, even better, to create a similar haven for yourself.

ABOVE

A blue, padded day-bed adorned
with cushions glows in the filtered
sunlight – the ideal setting for a
moment of glorious laziness.

RIGHT

The warm quality of wood,
the cheerfulness of the check
gingham and an imposing bed
create a comfortable atmosphere
in a traditional Alsatian house.

When people think of a room in a provincial house, they imagine a nest-like miniature island of calm where they can find refuge from the rough-and-tumble of the world, snuggle under a soft eiderdown with the peaceful abandon of a sleeping child, and renew their spirits. Everyone has his or her own reasons for liking a bedroom of a particular kind. Such rooms have an otherworldly quality. A favourite pleasure in them is choosing whether to close the shutters at the end of the day and reopen them as the new day begins, or to be able to contemplate the moon and stars from bed. Some people are captivated by the music and sounds of the world heard from their bedroom: the song of the nightingale, a morning chorus from mocking black-birds, creaking wood, the pitter-patter of rain on the roof, the whistling of the wind on winter nights, and muffled noises of other people in the house getting up while you are still tucked under the duvet. There may be a delicate joy of fragrances coming in through a window left open during the summer season: cut grass, hay, wisteria or climbing roses, lavender, lemon verbena or dried petals from wardrobes, unforgettable odours of apples and crab-apples spread on racks in the nearby loft. The sensual pleasures of the bedroom are by no means limited to the bed. But what is the true power of these provincial bed-rooms to be so enchanting? The answer may well be the same as for styles of regional architecture: their sheer affability – what the French call their *bonhomie*. They do not shout out, 'See how elegant I am!' but say simply, 'All is well'. In general, too, they are imbued with a feminine sensibility.

You leave your soft bed, and your bare feet touch the shimmering parquet floor or the glossy red hexagonal tiles. The walls may be hung with flowered wallpaper, and some-times covered with *toile de Jouy*, which seems exquisitely dated. More often than not, the furniture is rustic rather than sophisticated, and a thousand variations are possible. Beds may be enclosed or have a bedstead of turned wood, light or dark, while vast carved wardrobes bear the distinctive signs of regional furniture. You might also find

a more ornate four-poster bed or, influenced by nine-teenth-century Romanticism, bunk beds or even copper bedsteads draped with virginal white veils. Or plain divans may be perched in alcoves or under a sloping ceiling, half-hidden under the curtains.

Such beds may vary in age and value, but they will have one thing in common: their antique sheets and covers. These will be quilted feather eiderdowns in satin wraps, some-times re-covered with a white embroidered cloth; counter-panes; patched and often re-embroidered bed-throws; oriental spreads; mattresses; printed fabrics; sometimes traditional local cloth such as Provençal prints or Alsatian coverlets of linen, cotton or flax with distinctive weaves and colours that allow their owners to be identified.

The decoration of the bedroom is enhanced by a chest of drawers, a bedside table, a padded wing-chair or elabo-rately cushioned armchair, and those charming pieces forgotten by modern interior designers: writing desks, low

PREVIOUS DOUBLE-PAGE SPREAD
A Louis XVI cupboard holds the fragile linen and familiar knick-knacks belonging to the Château de Jozerand (left). Family photographs, a barley wreath and net curtains as delicate as spider's-webs grace an Alsatian house (right).

fireside-chairs and a dressing table. This is truly furniture to dream of and with; it might suit an adolescent girl sitting at the table to write her journal; or a kindly grandmother who draws up her low fireside-chair before the grate; or even a beautiful young woman who sets out her scent-bottles, face powder and powder-puff, hair-brushes and combs on her dressing table. In the evening, we can imagine her sitting before the mirror in her pretty underwear: perhaps she feels a little off-colour, so with a sigh of relief she unfastens her hair, removes her earrings and arranges her jewels in their precious box.

The windows are hung with net curtains, half-curtains, point-lace hangings and thick curtains with pelmets. The walls are decorated with mirrors, paintings and portraits, for bedrooms like this are the sanctuaries of family history and of time past. The chest of drawers, the bed-side tables and mantelpieces often bear an assortment of objects similar to that found in even the poorest country homes. There are likely to be carefully framed photographs, silver or silver-gilt christening presents, marriage veils and decorations under glass domes, little clocks, pieces of precious decorative china, and dried flowers.

Real treasures can be found in the enormous wardrobes in such bedrooms – or, more rarely, in the adjoining linen cupboards. Here the linen, folded and piled meticulously, bears witness to an age-old tradition. The quality will depend on income and status, but fine linen will certainly be part of a bride's trousseau. In the past, young girls would begin to embroider as soon as they could hold a needle. Cross-stitch, stem-stitch, hem-stitch on drawn cotton; in manipulating these arcane stitches young girls demonstrated their dexterity and their capacity to become perfect mistresses of their houses. It was important to mark their initials on the trousseau, to which they added the name of their future husband when their engagement was announced. The linen or flax was woven from local products by artisans, and sheets were often made of two pieces sewn together in the middle. The embroidery was invariably excellent, and even on sheets that had been repaired showed evidence of great artistry. These sheets had to be looked after very carefully, and were kept between perfumed sachets on wardrobe shelves. If an especially honoured guest was ever offered these sheets, he would have considered it an unmitigated pleasure, because no modern sheet, however luxurious, could match the freshness of these sheets of yesteryear.

LEFT
Minor details create a pleasing atmosphere in a peasant house: twin beds with iron bedsteads, neatly arranged bed-spreads, a sober bedside table, a Voltaire chair upholstered in a tapestry fabric, and walls covered with pictures.

ABOVE
At Pradié in the Aveyron, the bed is set in an alcove draped with hangings and covered with a valance which endows it with charm and a protective air. A bedcover was an essential part of a young countrywoman's trousseau in centuries past.

PAGES 114-115
Freshly plumped-up pillows,
hem-stitched sheets, a teapot
on the lace bedside-table cover:
the bedroom of Léonie, Marcel
Proust's aunt, at Illiers-Combray.

PAGES 116-117
Peasant furniture, stacks of
books and piles of magazines
and an accumulation of pictures
and objects of sentimental value:
the owner of this house has
collected, in his bedroom,
everything that summons
up the world of the Camargue
of a bygone era.

LEFT
A divan buried under draped
curtains: a personal and
self-contained space created
as a retreat for rest and
day-dreams, in a Rouergue
house.

RIGHT
The discreet and sober charm
of this corner basin adds serenity
to the bedroom.

PAGE 120
This original box-bed from
Brittany is one of the most
attractive pieces of furniture
in the Eco Museum on the Bretton
island of Ouessant.

PAGE 121
A folding bed that would not
look out of place in a monastery
is well suited to the minimalist
beauty of a shepherd's house in
Haute-Provence (Upper Provence).

LEFT-HAND PAGE
Pastel shades, a table covered
with a long cloth and snowy
pillows in a Provençal house.

RIGHT
A bedroom in the grand style
in the Château of Courance.
Elegant furniture and select
fabrics suit the mural decorations.

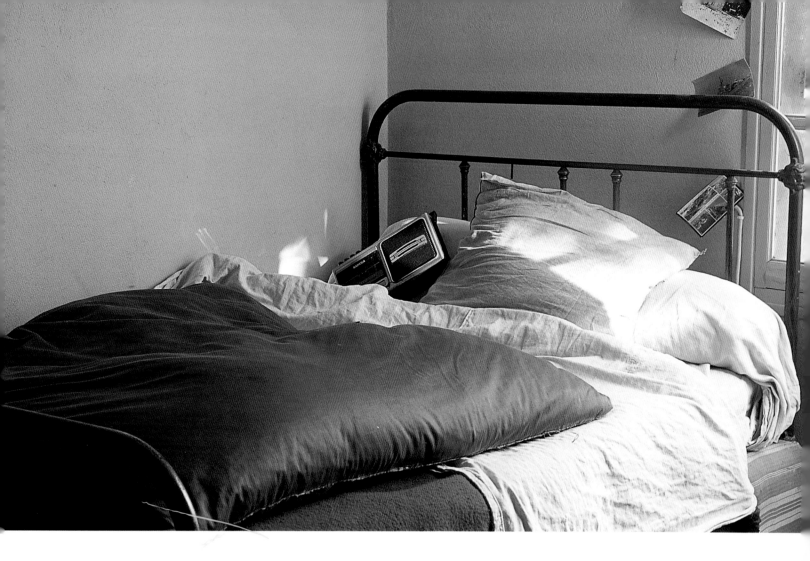

ABOVE
An old bed, covered with
a luxurious eiderdown,
in a farm in the Perigord.

RIGHT
A mixture of textiles –
Toile de Jouy, a patchwork
quilt and a flowered cushion
impart brightness and vigour
to a provincial house.

PAGES 126-127
Hung on the wall like a work
of art, the tender portrait and
accoutrements of a Provençal
grandmother (left).
A well-arranged wardrobe
belonging to a methodical
man who wants everything
to hand (right).

PAGES 128-129
The splendour of bygone days
in the Château de Jozerand:
the vast space of the linen room
is surrounded with cupboards
packed with treasures. In the
centre is a stove on which irons
were heated to press and smooth
the handsome linen belonging
to the house.

The pleasures
of the dining-room

The French art of living and respect for handed-down tradition come together when a household brings out its perfectly starched and ironed table-napkins and sparkling crystal glassware; when the variegated colours of bouquets of flowers are illuminated by candlelight; when the table is laid, and when the return journeys between kitchen and table become trips to fetch and carry miraculous dishes of sheer succulence. Of course, the organisers of these occasions, whether small, intimate celebrations or large-scale receptions, have traditionally been women, and each woman has her own ideas of how things should be done. She has her own recipes as well as knowledge and commonsense to apply to traditions inherited from her family. She hands them on — as if they were the most exquisite family secrets — to her daughters and sons.

ABOVE AND RIGHT
Toulouse-Lautrec exercised his
sense of humour at these tables
with their superb embroidered
tablecloths: he ordered goldfish
to be put in the carafes to
discourage the guests from
drinking water.

PAGES 134-135 AND 136-137
In dining-rooms, the open
cupboards display their
treasures and impeccable
arrays of precious glasses,
silverware and china dinner
services, plates, fish plates,
sauceboats, gravy boats and
soup bowls.

France may well be the only country in the world that has
raised the secrets of the 'Table' with a capital T to the status
of one of the key elements of its culture. The setting, rules
and know-how associated with a meal are displayed in
accordance with shared expectations. The rituals associated with eating have a sacred character. Although, with the
passage of time, the etiquette of dining has become much
less detailed and important, the social, family and celebratory occasions of life in France are still marked by
a gathering at the table. Eating together, and eating well,
remains one of the key events in national life. Formal
events elicit great care in choosing the most beautiful
objects available – whether linen, cutlery, glasses or silver
– for display and use. An elegant reception under the
chandeliers of a château, a wedding feast or a more modest
family party at a neighbouring farm proceed in essentially
the same way and observe the same basic proprieties. They
are all festive celebrations which combine good food and
wine, good cheer and conviviality. Even informal meals
have their own rules – there may be an occasional com-
promise with the strict demands of etiquette but they are
never abandoned completely.

In modern France, men play an increasingly greater part in
the preparations for a meal, and young boys are as likely as
their sisters to be asked to lay the table. However, the art of
the table is often still considered an especially feminine
domain. In the past, it would have been included automatically in the education of a 'well brought up' young lady.
She not only received a knowledge of, and instruction in,
entertaining from her mother but was also expected to
study it in detail, along with learning to play the piano,
sewing and embroidery. At the end of the seventeenth
century, the virtuous young ladies at the abbey of Saint-Cyr
were initiated into the arts of the table under the strict rule
of Madame de Maintenon. A household manual, *Mémento
Larousse, encyclopédique et illustré*, published at the begin-
ning of 1900, became one of the text-books handed to girls
preparing for their school-leaving certificate. It included
not only many pages devoted to history, geography,

mathematics, science, hygiene and so on, but also a chapter of 'practical advice on the art of living'. It contained recommended embroidery patterns and designs for table linen. Precise instructions were also given on how to issue an invitation, how to reply to one, how to dress for dinner, how to seat guests, how to arrange a menu in relation to one's budget, how to send dishes to table and lay it, 'A plate for each guest should be placed between the fork on the left and the knife on the right!... The table napkin placed on the plate or to its right should be folded in a straightforward way. The bread should be placed inside the napkin. A menu with the guest's name on it is to be placed in front of him or her.... A carafe of wine and a carafe of water should always be within reach of each male guest, whose duty it is to ensure that his female neighbour is served. A man is quite right to offer water to a woman, since it is generally agreed that women should drink very little wine.'

Choosing the appropriate tablecloth and table napkins has always been a serious business. These items are still traditionally considered indispensable in a young bride's trousseau. In the past, they had to be embroidered with the initials of both families, with predominance given to the young man's name, even if that meant interlacing initials. In the first half of the twentieth century, the expectation was that large numbers of such items were needed. At least a dozen tablecloths were considered necessary to cover all eventualities, and they should be of white cotton or linen for smart meals. Brittany was once the main centre of manufacture and weaving of linen and it produced such beautiful examples that they are now collector's pieces. It was usual to patronise regional textile producers from Brittany, or perhaps Alsace, when for instance, tablecloths for homely meals were required. Each tablecloth would be accompanied by its own collection of table napkins, never amounting to less than a dozen, while as many as two dozen would be ordered for ceremonial occasions.

In 1961, a French 'good housekeeping' manual made more modest recommendations, listing 'a large tablecloth of fine white material and twelve napkins, three smaller plain tablecloths and six assorted napkins for each table cloth; three cotton tablecloths for luncheon and six assorted table napkins to go with the tablecloth'. The following were cited for judicious use, 'white or pastel colours, in cambric, lawn, or organza cloth with inset lace or embroidered for traditional meals. Colour is to be used for an informal meal, but only one colour for an evening meal. In specifying a single colour, we do not mean embroidered or inset tablecloths but those with geometric or printed patterns, remembering that as a general rule floral patterns should

be kept for midday meals only. Never use a checked cloth for a celebratory meal'. These stipulations are not restricted to the choice of table linen, cutlery or seating arrangements for the guests, but also include detailed instructions as to the types of flowers and colours suitable for the flower arrangement to be placed on each table. Even in 1900, the recommendation was that 'a little flutter is not to be despised. There is no need to copy the expensive arrangements which would fill a princely table with orchids, even the most modest of households can buy some flowers in season or pick some greenery from the garden to add a lively note to the table.'

What has become of the dining-rooms of the past, their fine napery and exquisite china? They are still with us, fortunately, along with the classic dining-room furniture – table, chairs or benches, sideboard, dresser, butler's tray and dinner-wagon. The dining area, sometimes now, merely a designated corner of a living-room, is still an indispensable part of a French household. A leading

PAGES 138-139
More modest arrangements are no
less attractive. Everything needed
to make a meal is within reach, as
is a sometimes charming mixture
of crockery and clothing.

ABOVE
In the dining-room of a Provençal
château, below an array of
chandeliers, a fine silk brocade
tablecloth perfectly matches
the colour of the walls and the
central flower arrangement.

RIGHT
A simple lunch in a traditional
house in the Aveyron – plain
yet elegant furniture, a place
setting for each guest, stout
earthenware plates, a bottle
of wine and a jug of fresh water.

DOUBLE-PAGE SPREAD overleaf
A blindfold wine-tasting at
a château in the Bordelais
region; a traditional custom
in all wine-growing areas.

expert, Jacques Puisais, the founder of the *L'Institut français du goût* (French Institute of Good Taste), has defined the ideal setting for meals as 'concordant walls painted or decorated in soft, neutral colours complemented by adequate though non-aggressive lighting which must not give an unnatural colour to food or wine, and, of course, a peaceful and relaxed atmosphere'.

In France, one can still find interior-decorating magazines featuring long articles on table decorations and settings, on choosing fine dinner services and tablecloths, and also commenting on innovations in the field. If people have not been lucky enough to inherit suitably fine antiques, they must comb the growing number of second-hand stalls and specialist antique shops. The elaborate etiquette of the past has almost vanished but a concern for excellent cuisine at one's own table still exists, and most people are happy to spend time and effort in its pursuit, pondering over tableware and china until the right mix is achieved, trying out table decorations and settings, juxtaposing old and new, and attending to points of detail. From the right

glasses to appropriate candles and suitable flowers, it is understood that one must balance the desire for a beautiful scene, that would rival the most conscientious of restaurants, against the requirement of a setting that encourages easy sociability. We no longer await the formal announcements of servants before entering the dining-room, but the invitation by the host to proceed to the table leads us to one of the great pleasures afforded by the art of French country living.

ABOVE AND RIGHT
Whether at a fireside dinner
in a house in the provinces,
or at a more formal reception
in a magnificent setting, an
attractively laid table not only
starts guests talking but also
whets their appetites.

LEFT AND ABOVE
Carefully chosen and planned
lighting is one of the elements
of the art of entertaining.
Chandeliers and candelbra
aid the atmosphere of this
dining-room in a château
in the Gers.

RIGHT
An elaborate oil-lamp,
a nineteenth-century
metalwork creation, illuminated
the Proust family's dining-room
at Illiers-Combray.

DOUBLE-PAGE SPREAD *overleaf*
A nineteenth-century innovation
to ensure that dishes remained
hot was plate-warmers integrated
in radiators.

ABOVE AND RIGHT
In a rustic farmhouse as in
an early twentieth-century
middle-class home, a white
tablecloth is always synonymous
with elegance and conviviality.

RIGHT
A formally laid table in a large
dining-room in the Château du
Bosc, Aveyron, as Henri de
Toulouse-Lautrec would have
known it when he was a child.

PAGES 152-153
The small dining-room at the
Château du Bosc is next to the
kitchen and enabled the family
to entertain their guests in an
intimate family setting.

PAGES 154-155 AND 156-157
Although menus scarcely ever appear in private houses today, the art of the table is an opportunity for the mistress of the house to give free rein to her creativity, both in the choice and arrangement of tableware and by the selection of delights to please her guests' palates.

LEFT, RIGHT AND PAGES 159-160
The arts of the table are often evoked or described in French literature. Here the illustrations of different scenes from the world of Proust range from the Château de Guermantes to Madame Verdurin's famous potato salad.

ABOVE AND RIGHT
At Giverny, Claude Monet's
dining-room was the scene of
an exacting ritual, established by
the painter himself. At Christmas,
the champagne was decanted into
a carafe, and a pudding in the
French style followed the
numerous courses.

DOUBLE-PAGE SPREAD *overleaf*
Every year at Monet's festive
table, each child would find an
envelope containing a gift by
his or her plate.

The joys of the kitchen

The joys of the kitchen are enjoyed not only
at meals but also at any time on an incidental
visit to the kingdom of good food. Here, prime
consideration is given not only to the quality of
the ingredients but also to their careful cooking.
Kitchens take on the identity of their owners.
You might be reluctant to leave an easy-going,
reassuring country kitchen for one attached to
a prestigious château, but even the grandest
are more likely to prove hospitable than
supercilious. The most irresistible kitchens
are those that appear to have been created as
models for all time. They are redolent of the
taste and creativity of great artists and gourmets
such as Claude Monet and Marcel Proust.
In such fine kitchens, favourite dishes are
served up with other culinary masterpieces
inseparable from regional French culture.
So much so that it is a tautology to add the
word 'French' to the term 'gastronomy'.

Now the door opens on that sanctuary, the kitchen. The French word *cuisine* comes from the Latin *coquere*, 'to cook', but by extension it soon came to designate the room where food is prepared. The kitchen was originally the very centre of the household, the location of the fire to which was owed not only light and heat, but food cooked rather than raw, the foundation of human culture and civilisation. Our prehistoric ancestors gathered round the hearth to keep warm. At first it would have been little more than a simple hole in the ground: archaeologists in the Dordogne have found blackened stones apparently used to grill the animals captured by hunters. Later fragile walls were built around these fires and makeshift roofs with an opening for the smoke to escape. Then the hearth became a shelter for the family or clan, its unique living space, the common room to which, very gradually, other rooms were added. Words such as 'hearth' (*foyer* in French) soon referred to more than the space where the fire (and later the oven) was placed, and became laden with meaning. It became synonymous with 'household', and eventually took on a sociological dimension as the place where a family lived. The word *foyer* is still used to refer to the family itself.

Not all country kitchens have preserved their hearth, that magical alcove where people gathered on the cold evening, and where food was cooked, exuding aromas that aroused the appetites of all – even the gastronomic dullards. Nevertheless a kitchen is still the warm heart of the home, cherished as much for its atmosphere as for the dishes prepared there.

RIGHT
The work-surfaces and shelves of this rustic Provençal kitchen allow the main utensils and condiments to be kept within easy reach.

Traditional kitchens are rooms to be used, and are redolent of kinship and fellowship in every household, whether a manor house or a simple country cottage or farmhouse. The streamlined, chrome-plated, stainless-steel and coolly-ordered modern style of kitchen is a world apart from the endearing disorder, wood, old tiles, woven baskets and pottery of the old-fashioned kitchen. The dressers and shelves of these authentic kitchens are crammed with stoneware pots, terrines, glazed earthenware, bread-baskets and jars. Here, wire crates full of vegetables and fruits from the garden or market offer frank displays of their fresh treasures. There are also bread-boxes and bins, chests, buffets, cupboards, larders with squeaking doors and big tables of solid wood. They are all permeated with the mixed fragrances of apples, bread, honey and jams.

These kitchens are not just used occasionally but are true living rooms. The family congregates here for breakfast or informal meals. They are ideal places for a break or a snack, a cold sausage washed down with a glass of chilled wine. They are natural family meeting-places where peaceful conversation is encouraged. Sometimes, guests may offer to help with the preparations, and their offer may well be accepted. As the writer Philippe Delerm testified in his moving account of shelling peas in *La première gorgée de bière et autres plaisirs minuscules* (The first mouthful of beer and other minor pleasures): 'Breakfast bowls and crumbs are now forgotten, and the lingering fragrances of lunchtime distant memories. The kitchen is so calm and almost abstract that the question, "Do you need any help?" is utterly natural. As soon as you sit down at the family table a sense of peace descends on you as you begin to shell the peas mechanically, an action whose very rhythm seems dictated by some inner metronome. The sentences you utter are unforced and intermittent, and in that kitchen the music of the words, peaceful and familiar, seems to come from within.'

The kitchen is the room on which all the conviviality of a French house depends. It is a veritable alchemist's crucible for boiling, roasting and simmering a multitude of succulent delights ranging from a boiled egg to the most elaborate of dishes. One of the most renowned characteristics of the French is their profound interest in food and its preparation. This is no new phenomenon. A Gallo-Roman poet born in Bordeaux in the fourth century AD, by name of Ausonius, was a gastronomic critic and inventor of recipes with a refined dietary repertoire. In 1380, Taillevent, the head cook of Charles VI of France, wrote his *Viandier de Paris* (a Parisian treatise on victuals),

one of the first cookery books. The works of the sixteenth-century satirical writer Rabelais, himself a leading patron of the table, included an account of 'galligutted gastro-laters'. In 1535, Michel de Nostre-Dame (better known as Nostradamus) published a book on jams and preserves – his recipes are delicious. The list goes on to include such figures as Madame de Sévigné, a great letter-writer who was also at times an excellent food writer, and nineteenth-century authors like Alexandre Dumas who wrote a *Dictionary of Cuisine*, Emile Zola, Guy de Maupassant, Gustave Flaubert, Edmond Rostand who wrote marvellous descriptions of love-feasts, Marcel Proust, the Goncourt brothers, and Brillat-Savarin and his *Physiologie du goût* (Physiology of Taste). Then, of course, there were also famous cooks such as Marie-Antoine Carême and Escoffier.

Modern France is no different. Philosophers, sociologists and literary figures like Antoine Blondin and Colette often write about food or slip their favourite recipes into their works or letters. The extraordinary volume, *Cuisine paléolithique* (Palaeolithic Cuisine) by artist Joseph Delteil, probably did more for a return to simple food and genuine, unadulterated products and tastes than a host of dietary manuals, and many modern works have as their subject-matter the choice recipes of a famous author.

Today, a love of good food is more evident than ever before. As Maguelonne Toussaint-Samat remarks, with a touch of caustic humour, in his *Histoire naturelle de la nourriture* (The History of Food): 'The gastronomy of which France is so proud has a sense of religious denomination: popes (such as the late Brillat-Savarin); bibles (just survey the cookery shelves of any general bookshop in France); choirmasters who orchestrate new culinary tastes; and merchants in the temple who cut costs and produce cheap imitations.' But where does French home cooking fit in?

On the whole, the situation in the French countryside is very good even though its homes are not necessarily uniquely endowed with culinary skills. Perhaps this is because people there have more time available than those harassed by urban stresses and so they emphasize the whole ritual of food and cooking more effectively. Above all, they love to talk about food. The day's menus are discussed and debated with a gourmet's passion at French country breakfast tables.

Later, the ideas become reality, and although many modern recipes use ingredients originating in other cuisines – a practice to which no one could object – traditional cooking and an emphasis on local products remain

ABOVE
A simple meal - an open bottle of wine awaits the guests and the soup is cooking on the stove in this kitchen in the Béarn.

RIGHT
Every home has a larder or place to keep dairy products and cheeses cool.

PAGES 172-173
When the heat is off in the oven,
the hotplate can double as a work-
top while the meal is prepared.

PAGES 174-175
Finely chopped onions, crushed
garlic, neatly diced aubergines,
peppers, courgettes and tomatoes
are cooked separately and then
mixed together with thyme and
bay leaf. Attention to detail is
vital when making an authentic
ratatouille.

the first choice. No decent home would hesitate to offer visiting friends the best of their area's specialities: an 'authentic' Toulouse cassoulet, with genuine Aveyron tripe, the inimitable chard tart in the style of Nice, an Aubrac stew of turkey giblets, or a traditional Breton fish soup. Any caring host would automatically serve the delicacies, butter and specialities of the area; its cheeses and, if it is a wine-growing area, a good local vintage; fresh eggs from the neighbouring farm, spectacular French runner beans, lettuces and tomatoes from the garden or bought from the best local producer.

Flavours, tastes and passions of the palate, as well as of the heart, are celebrated in concert in French country kitchens, where cooking, as that lover of good food, Colette, said, implies 'a clear head, a generous spirit and a big heart'. And what could be more French that that?

LEFT AND ABOVE

Whether it's plain and functional or grand and splendid, the kitchen is always the living heart of the house. In the room shown above the chandelier and handsome furniture go very well with the impressive 'cook's piano' beneath the chimney hood (as the traditional stove is sometimes known in France).

PAGE 178
Little girls love to play with the dough when the cook is making puddings for the family.

PAGE 179
This magnificent pyramid cake is a speciality of the Aveyron. It is cooked before the fire, and its shape comes from arranging the dough skilfully around a central wooden support.

PAGES 180-181 AND LEFT
A cook's pots and pans should not be hidden. Hanging or standing in studied disorder on a set of plain wooden shelves, they add a homely touch to the magic of a room.

RIGHT
The fireplace is a source of warmth and vitality in a kitchen, whether in a château or in a simple country home.

The kitchens that remain in our
memory are those that seem like
temples in which to celebrate the
love of good food cooked in the
traditional way. At Illiers-Combray
(pages 184-185), Marcel Proust's
kitchen houses an evocative array
of casseroles, cooking pots and
frying pans.
Monet's kitchen at Giverny
(pages 186-187) was always
one of the most important
rooms in the house.

LEFT
This stilton soup is served in a
traditional tureen.

RIGHT
Kept by his cook, Monet's
recipe book was important
for the painter, who was an
enthusiastic host.

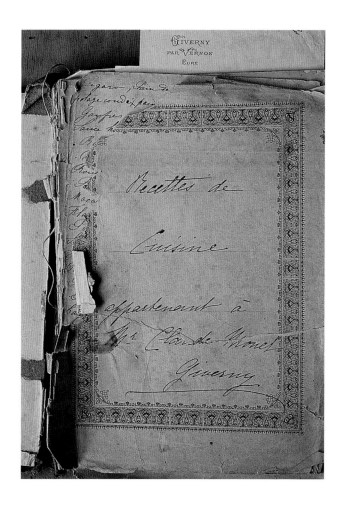

DOUBLE-PAGE SPREAD overleaf
Vegetables and fruit wait in a cool
corner of the kitchen in the Béarn
region (page 190); Provençal tomatoes
sizzling in a Camargue kitchen give
off a rich fragrance (page 190); chunks
of pork roast on a spit and gently drip
onto bread slices which become totally
saturated, in the style of the Ariège
(pages 192-193); fresh foie gras is fried
over a wood fire in the Gers (page 194),
while the crème catalane caramelises
under a red-hot iron (page 195) - just a
few tasters of the vast multitude of
French regional dishes.

PAGES 196-197
A round country loaf kept carefully
in a kitchen-table drawer offers
the most appropriate and simple way
of warding off hunger and satisfying
the appetite.

Pause for reflection

The greatest pleasure of life in the country is taking a walk. A walk may start your day or close it, precede a meal or follow it. It can clear your head and calm your heart, bewitch your vision with a palette of colours, beguile your sense of smell with scents, and intrigue your ears with the delicate music of rustling leaves and chattering birds. As you pause on your peaceful journey among the country pleasures of France, you recognise a house where time stands still beneath the climbing plants, the glistening pool, the water lilies, the gentle pathways, the delightful nooks, the flowering arches, and the nasturtiums dancing amidst splendid disorder. Only a great artist could have created a garden like this, where he loved to do his own sowing and planting as he created a living work of art stamped with his own special genius.

LEFT AND FOLLOWING
DOUBLE-PAGE SPREAD
Claude Monet's garden and house in Giverny, a place to observe the rhythm of the seasons.

Further reading

The French Country House, Christiane De Nicolay-Mazery, Bernard Touillon (Vendome, 2004)

French Garden Style, Ines Heugel (Hachette Illustrated, 2004)

Something to Declare, Julian Barnes (Picador, 2002)

Provence Style of Living, Jerôme Coignard (Hachette Illustrated, 2004)

The French Touch: Decoration and Design in the Most Beautiful Homes of France, Daphne De Saint Sauveur (Bulfinch Press, 1997)

Really Rural: Authentic French Country Style, Marie-France Boyer (Thames and Hudson, 1997)

New French Country: A Style and Source Book, Linda Dannenberg, Guy Bouchet (Thames and Hudson, 2004)

French Country Living, Caroline Clifton-Mogg (Ryland Peters & Small, 2004)

The French Country Garden, Louisa Jones et al (Thames and Hudson, 2000)

Recipes from Monet's Kitchen, Christine Grenard (Cassell Illustrated, 2000)

Acknowledgements

Every book has a history. This one represents the end of a long journey.
My warmest thanks go to Philippe Pierrelée
and to Isabelle Jendron whose patience and friendship throughout the
creation of this book, especially in the final stages, I value immensely.
I also want to thank all those people who have shown me their houses
so trustingly and given me permission to photograph them.
Finally, I am most grateful to François Huertas and Cécile Beaucourt
for putting up with me even when I was difficult to live with.

Jean Naudin

The French publishers, *Editions du Chêne*, and the photographer would like
to thank:
Mme Annie de La Celle, M. Bernard Dufour (Le Pradié), Mme Zéline Guéna
(Fort de Flaujagues), Mme Annie Laurent Manadière (Mas les Marquises),
the de Ligneris family (Château Soutard), M. Dominique Maurice,
Mlle Rosa Naudin, M. and Mme Jean and Dorothée d'Orgeval, Mrs Pillsbury,
Mr and Mrs Rendell, Mme Nathalie Romatet (Château Miromesnil),
Mr and Mrs Anthony Roberts, M. Jean de Rohan-Chabot (Château Jozerand),
Mme Nicole Tapié de Céleyran (Château Bosc, Toulouse-Lautrec's house),
Mrs Barbara Wirth (Château Brécy), the mayor and council of Aix-en-Provence
(Cézanne's studio and the Jas de Bouffan), Monet's house at Giverny, the
Renoir museum at Cagnes-sur-Mer, the owners of La Boissierette,
the owners of Mas Cacharel, of Castelas farm, of the Château and park of
Courances, of La Kibola and of Château Montvert, and all those who agreed
to our publishing photographs of their properties.

Editing: Cécile Beaucourt, assisted by Florence Renner
Design: François Huertas for PIKAONE
Proofreading: Isabelle Macé
Photogravure: APS/CHROMOSTYLE, Tours

First published by Editions du Chêne, an imprint of Hachette-Livre
43 Quai de Grenelle, Paris 75905, Cedex 15, France
Under the title *Une France Intime*.
© 2004, Editions du Chêne-Hachette Livre

English language translation produced by Translate-A-Book, Oxford

This edition published by Hachette Illustrated UK, Octopus Publishing Group,
2–4 Heron Quays, London, E14 4JP
English Translation © 2005, Octopus Publishing Group Ltd, London

Printed by Toppan Printing Co., (HK) Ltd.
ISBN-13: 978-1-84430-145-4
ISBN-10: 1-84430-145-1